Rosie and the Dinosaurs

Written by Julia Jarman
Illustrated by Julie Park

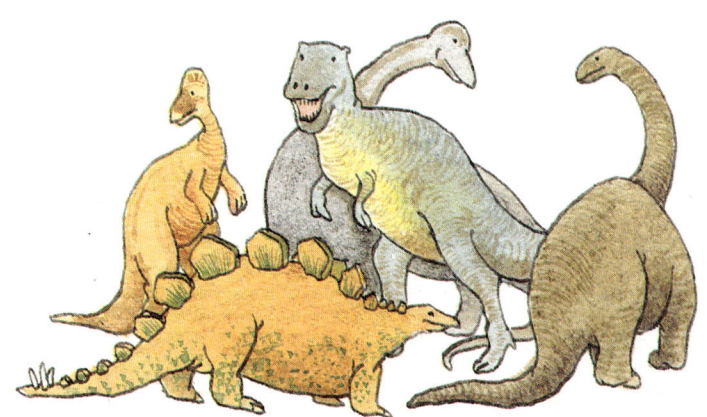

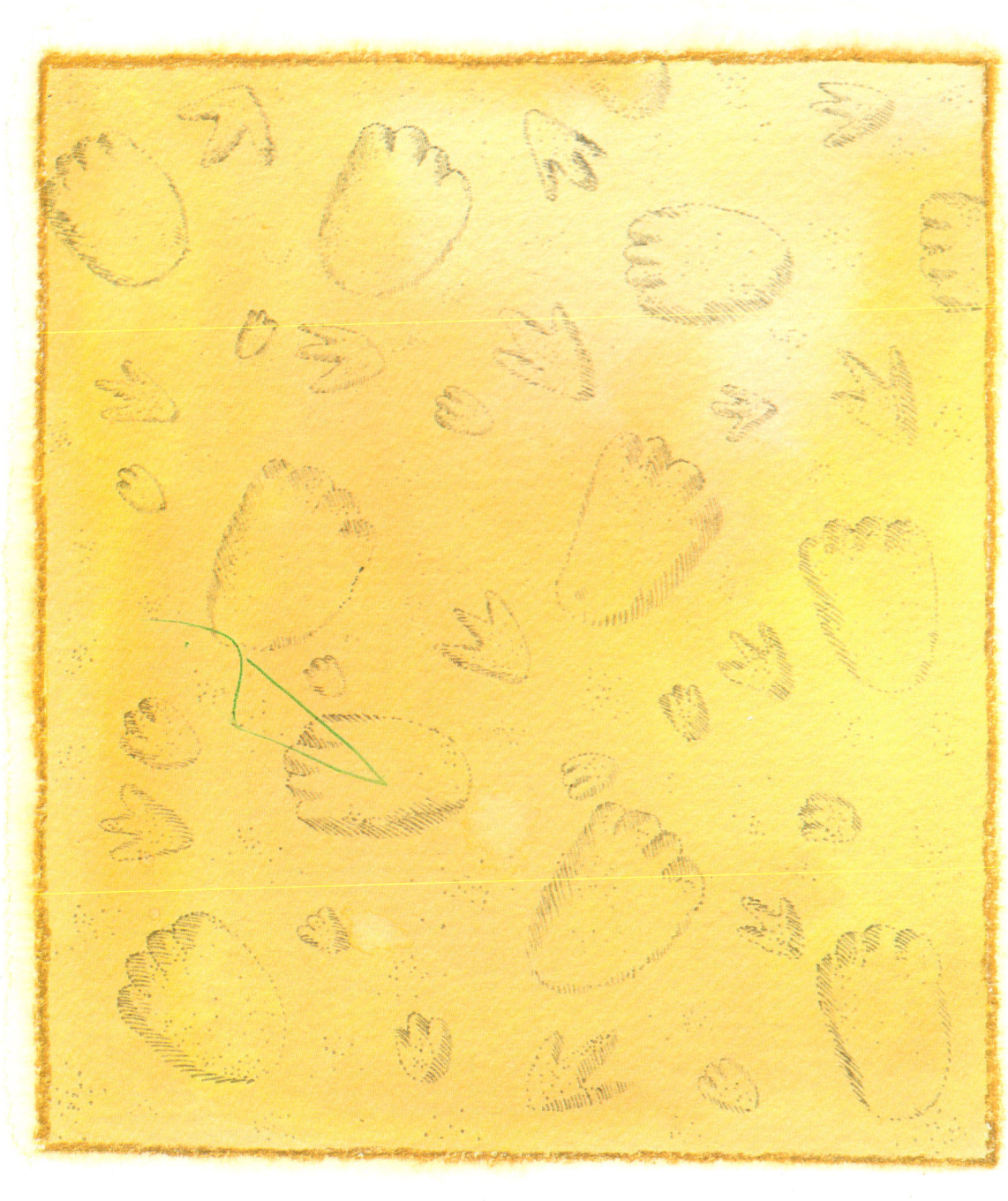

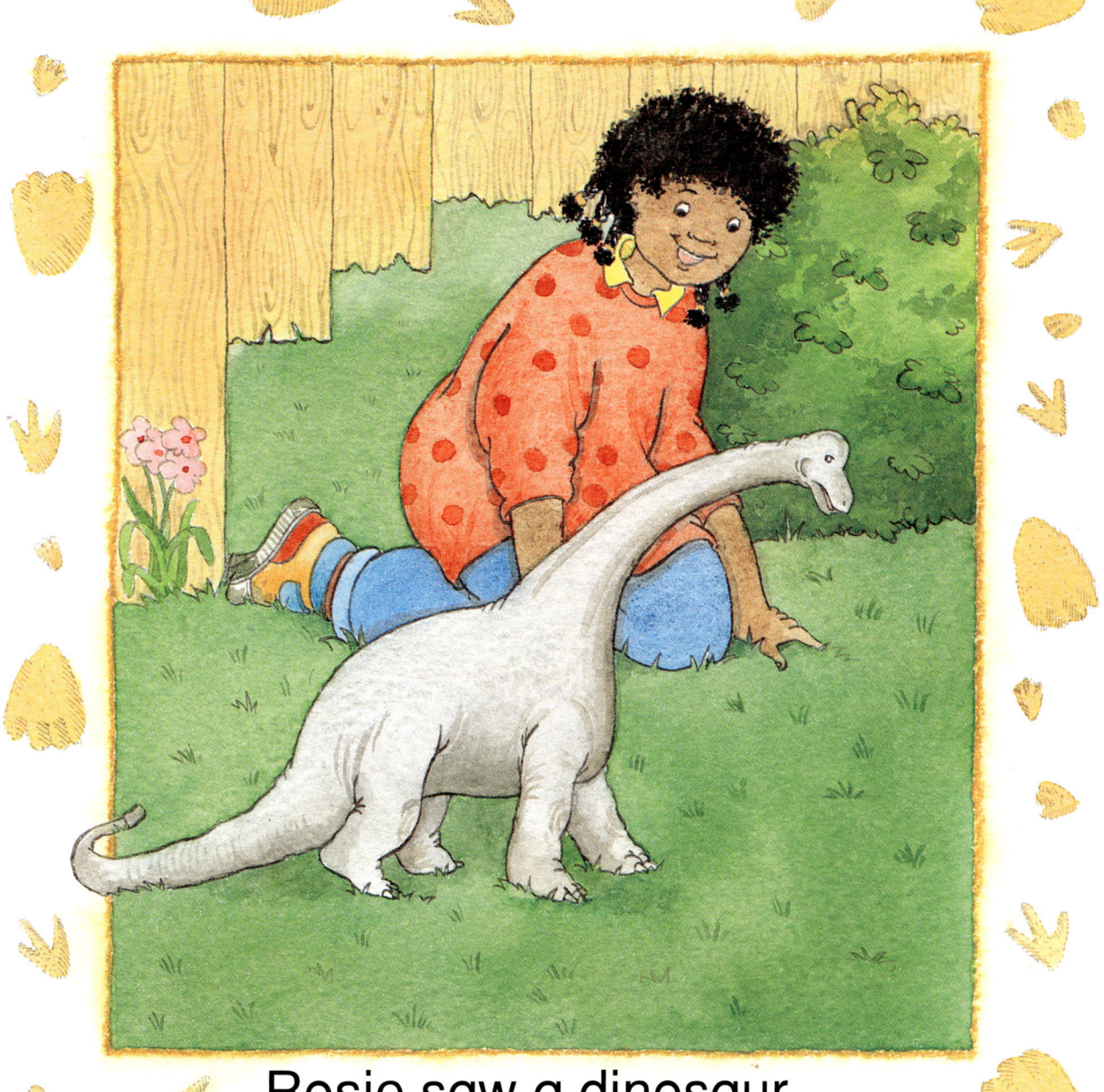

Rosie saw a dinosaur.

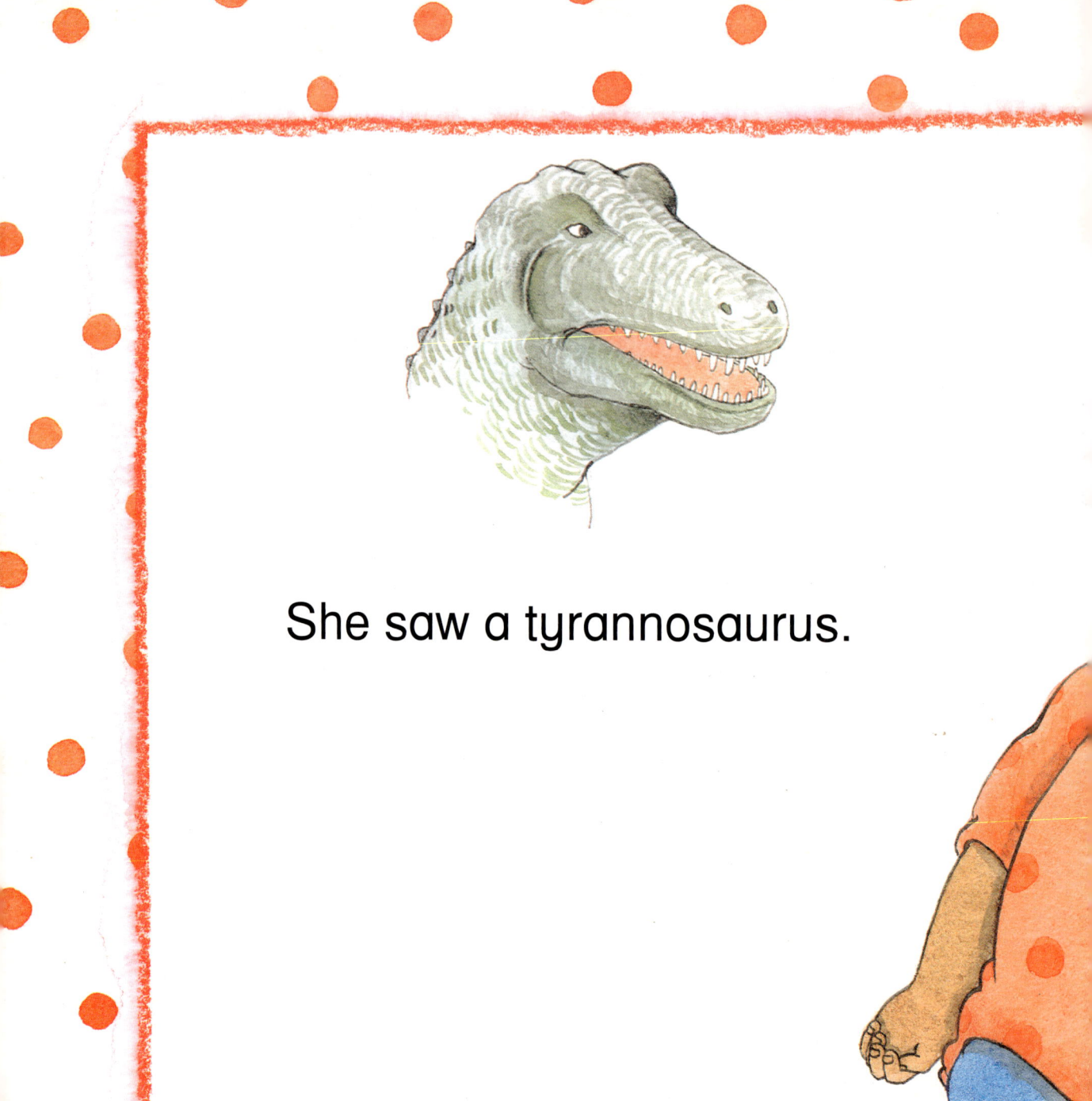

She saw a tyrannosaurus.

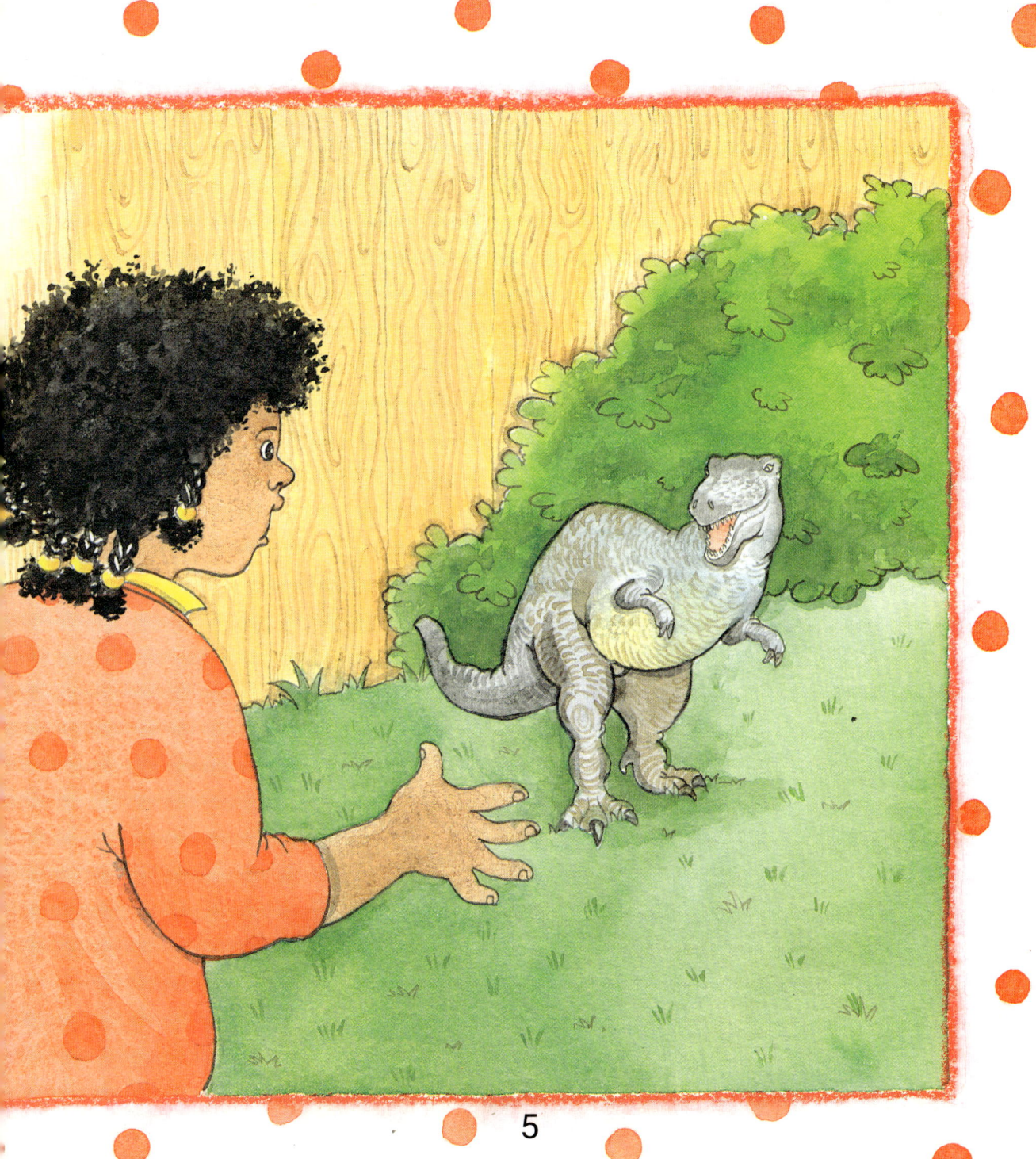

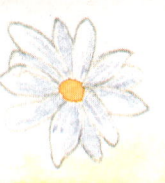
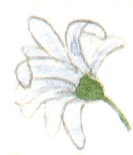

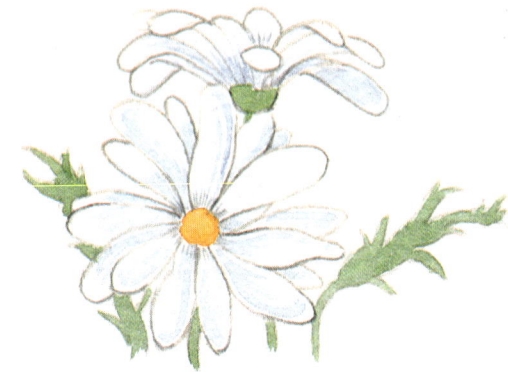
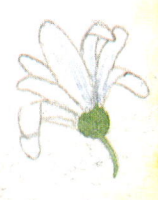

She saw a corythosaurus.

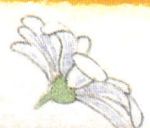

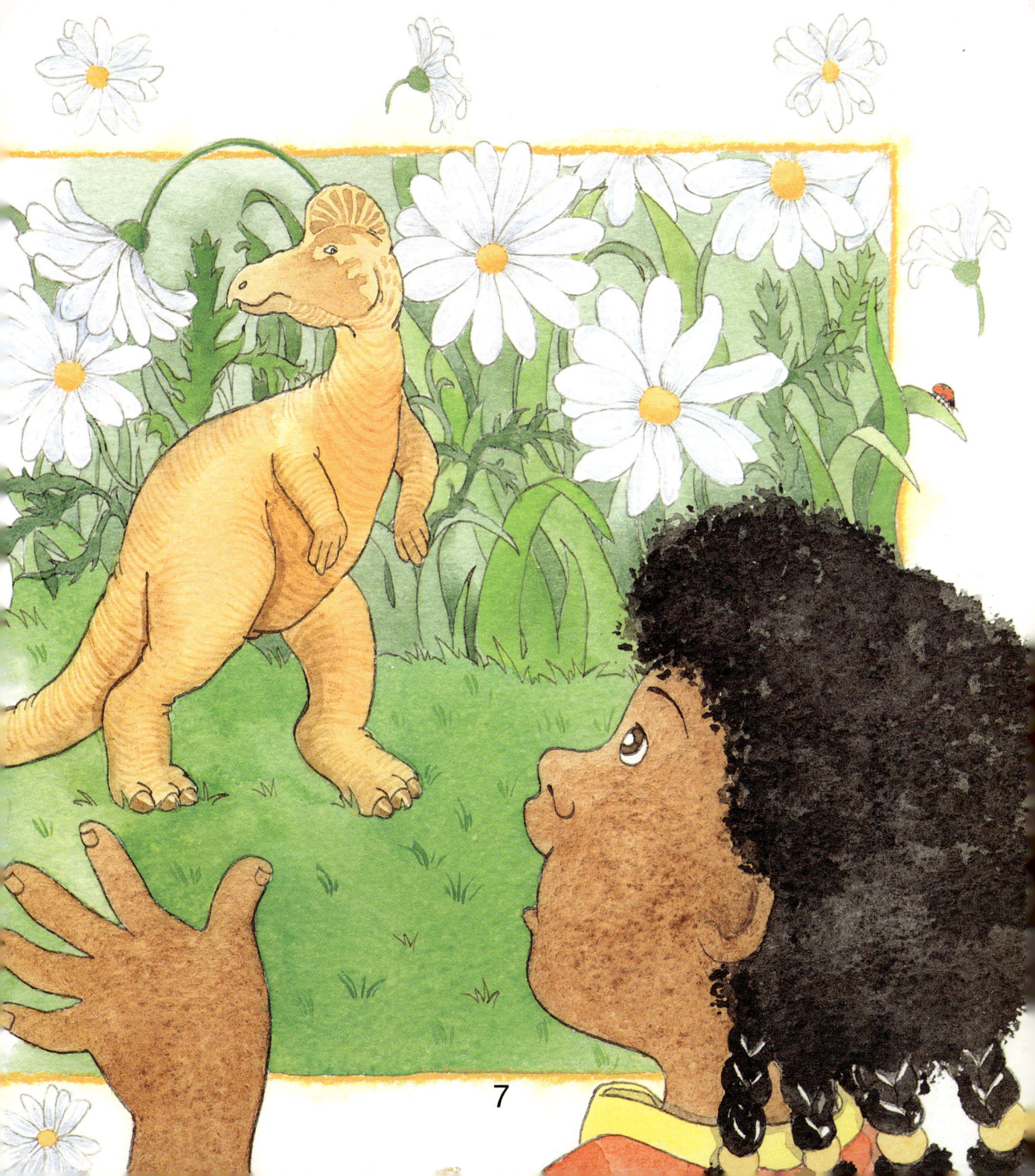

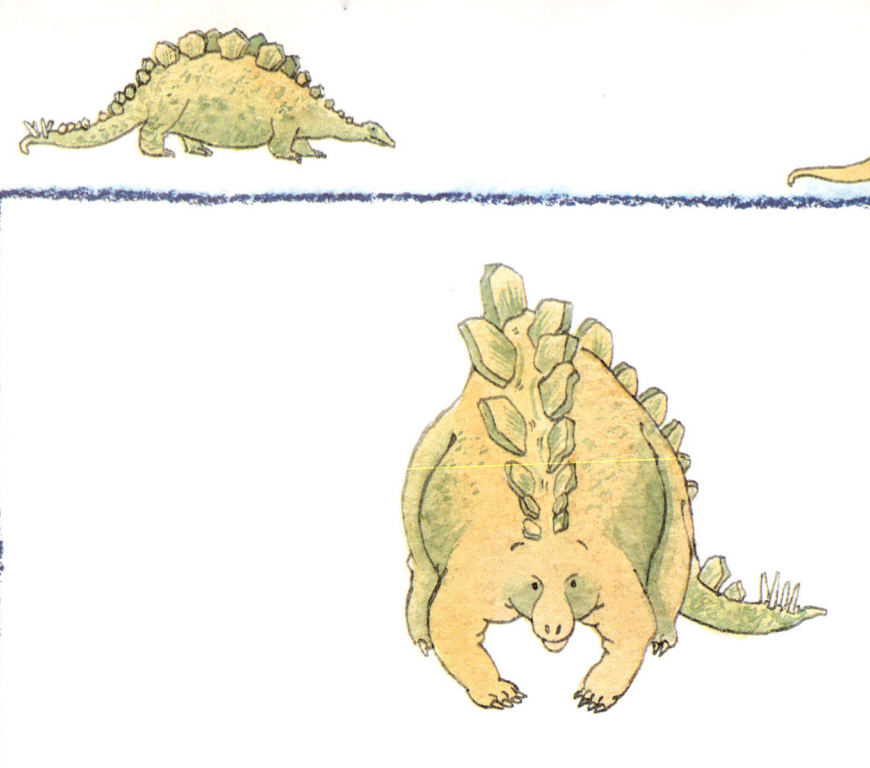

She saw a stegosaurus.

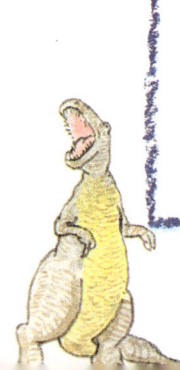
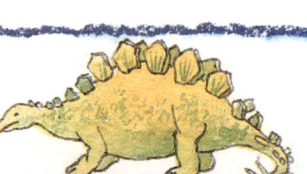

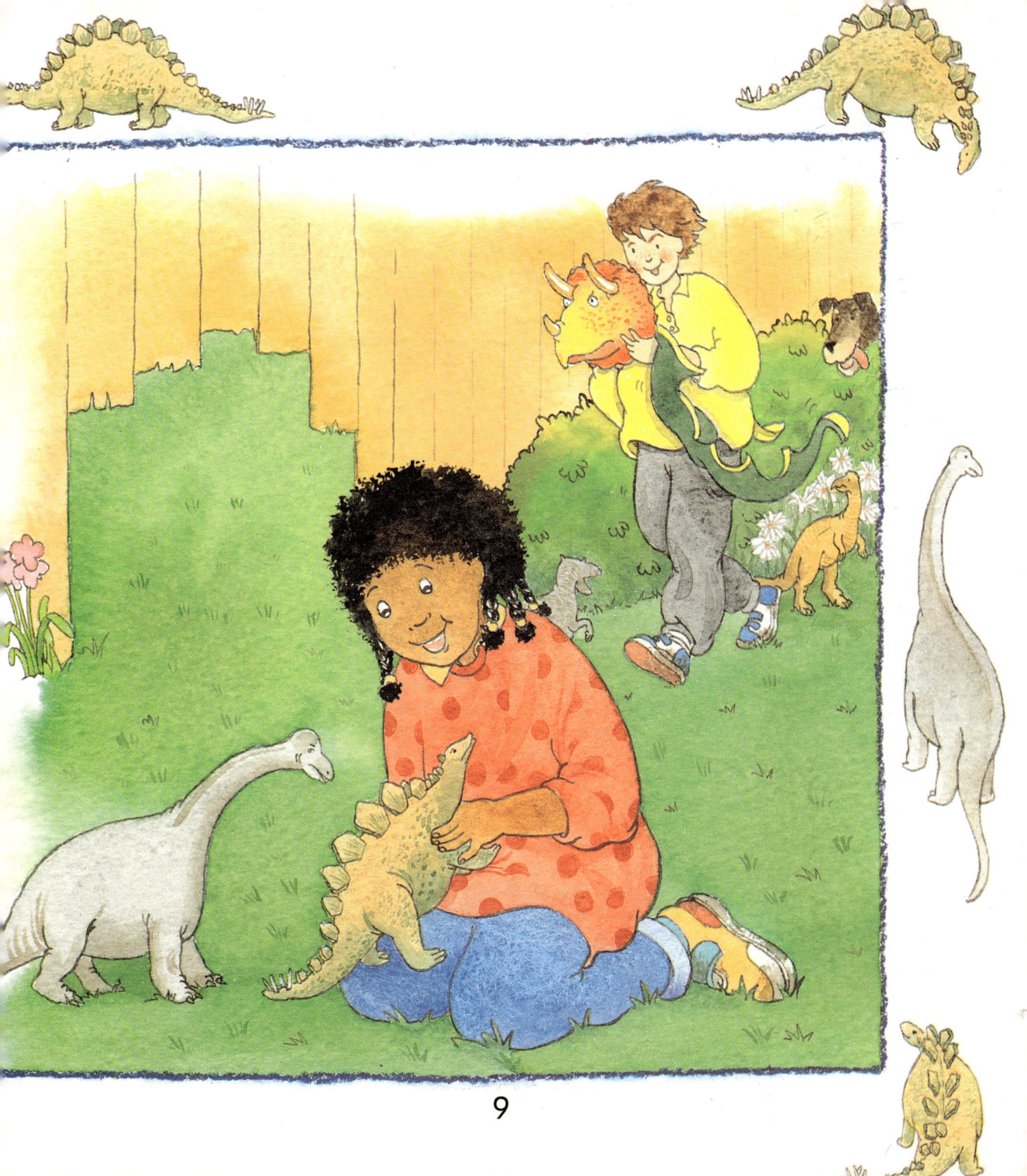

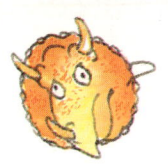
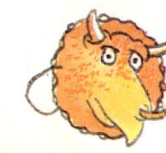
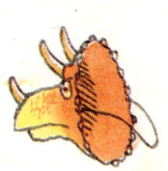
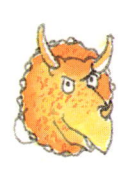
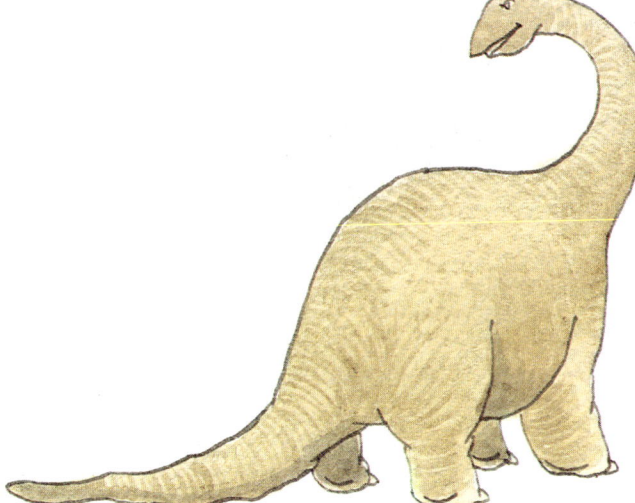

She saw an apatosaurus.

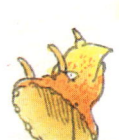
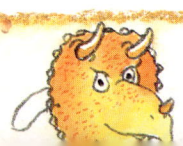

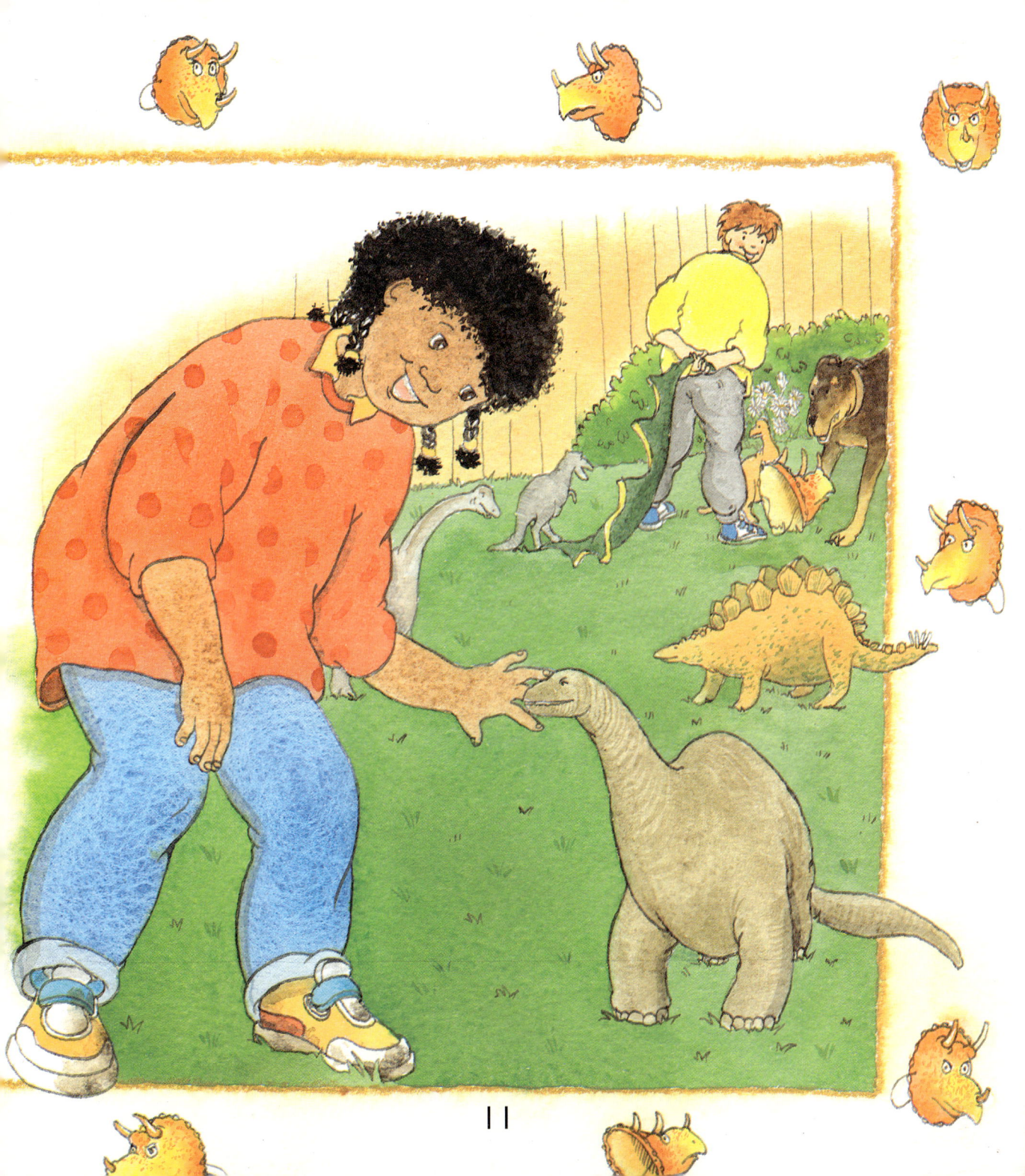

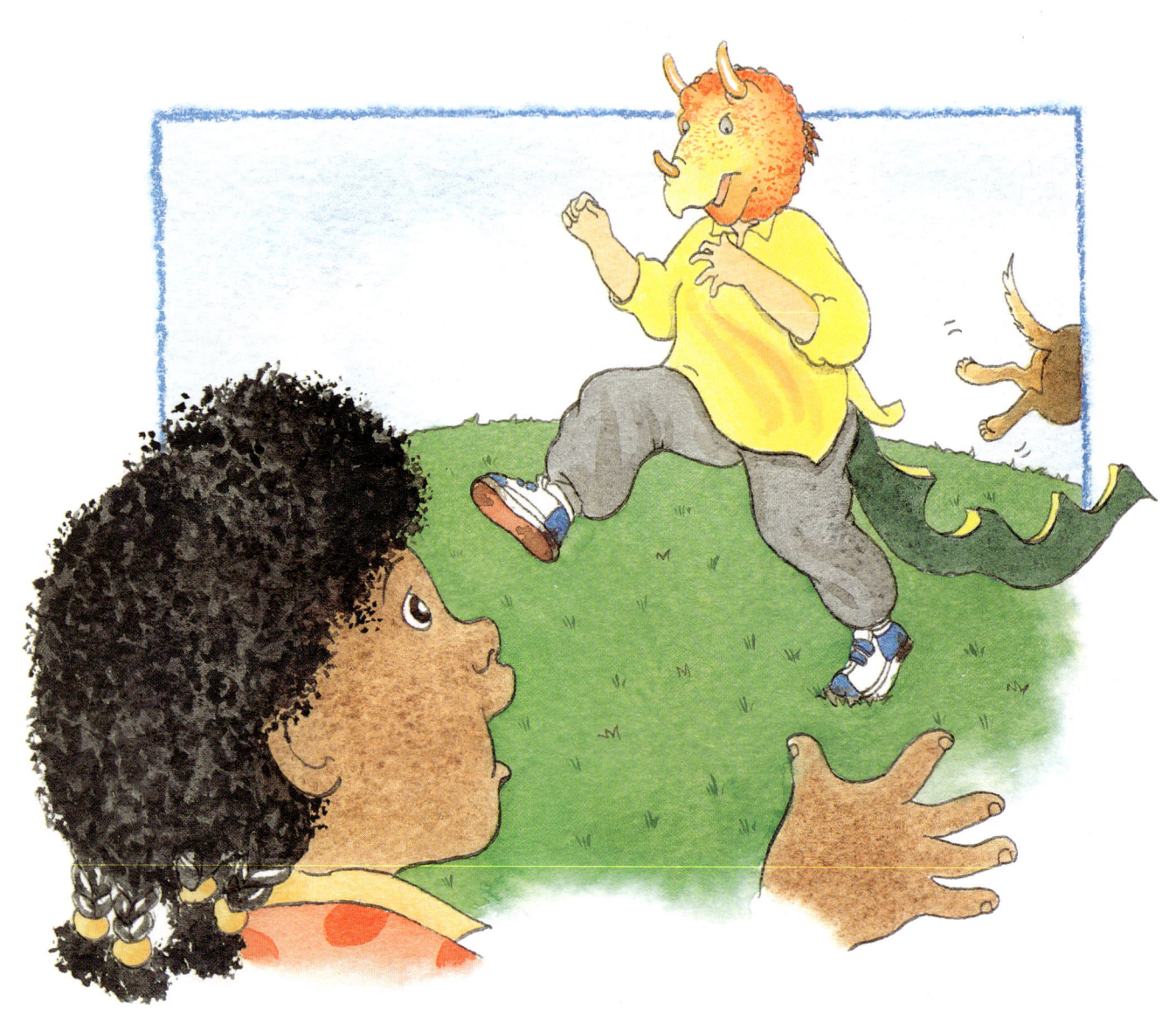

She saw a Samosaurus!